MOCHI

MOCHI

SABRINA FAUDA-RÔLE
PHOTOGRAPHY BY DAVID JAPY
ILLUSTRATIONS BY VALENTINE FERRANDI

Smith
Street
Books

CONTENTS

12

CHOCOLATE HAZELNUT SPREAD

14

CARAMELISED WALNUT

16

DANGO

18

SPECULOOS

20

HONEY ROSE ALMOND

22

ORANGE BLOSSOM APRICOT

26

RASPBERRY ICE CREAM

28

SESAME

30

CHOCOLATE

32

STRAWBERRY

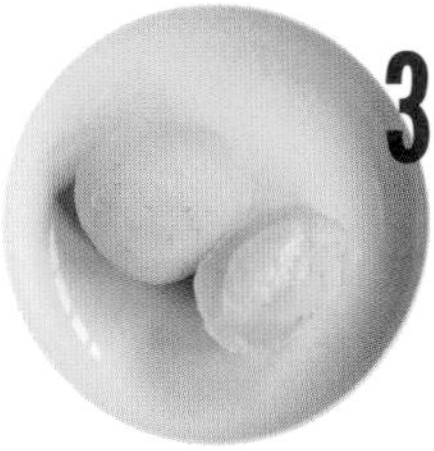

34

LEMON

38

VANILLA

40

PEANUT BUTTER JELLY

42

HAZELNUT AND CHESTNUT

44

ANKO MOCHI

46

BLUEBERRY LEMON

48

COCONUT MANGO

50

MATCHA COCONUT

52

PRALINE COFFEE

56

BLACK SESAME MATCHA

58

PASSIONFRUIT

60

ICE CREAM MOCHI

INGREDIENTS

A soft, elastic and sticky dough

A melt-in-your-mouth, sweet filling, often frozen

Fresh fruit, sometimes whole or in small pieces

BEST SERVED

Mochi are best served and eaten immediately (except for frozen mochi), but they can be enjoyed up to 48 hours after making. After this time, they will dry and harden.

TOOLS TO USE

1 bowl
1 whisk
1 chopping board

Mochi
TUTORIAL
IN 5 STEPS

Prepare the filling.

1

Shape the filling.

Prepare the mochi dough.

3

Fill and shape the mochi.

4

Leave the mochi to rest before eating.

5

Mochi dough

MAKES 12 MOCHI	
PREP TIME 15 MINUTES	
COOK TIME 2½ MINUTES	

150 g (5½ oz) glutinous rice flour

120 g (4½ oz) sugar

1 pinch of salt

200 ml (7 fl oz) cold water

cornflour (cornstarch) or potato starch for rolling

 In a microwave-safe bowl, mix the glutinous rice flour, sugar and salt. Gradually add the cold water, stirring constantly so as not to create lumps. If using food colouring, now is the time to add it, drop by drop, to achieve the desired colour. Note that the colour darkens when cooked.

 Cover the bowl with a lid or plastic wrap and place it in the microwave for 1 minute at maximum power. Stir lightly with a spatula. Cover and cook in the microwave for another 1 minute. Stir again, cover and return to the microwave for 30 seconds.

3 Sprinkle a work surface with cornflour. Place the still-hot dough on the work surface and sprinkle it with a thin layer of cornflour.

4 **2 OPTIONS:**

- Form the dough into a sausage of about 30 cm (12 in) in length then cut the dough into 40 g (1½ oz) pieces.

- Slide the dough between your thumb and forefinger (dust your hands well with cornflour), then pinch strongly and detach the piece of dough to form a small ball of about 40 g (1½ oz).

5 With hands dusted with cornflour, lightly squash the dough ball between your hands to form a 6–7 cm (2½–2¾ in) disc. Place a very cold ball of filling in the centre and quickly gather the edges on top of the ball by pinching them together to seal. Quickly roll the resulting ball between your hands to even it out and place it on a plate, seam side down.

6 Repeat to form the remaining mochi, then place them in the fridge to let them cool.

The dough can also be prepared in a saucepan by mixing the ingredients over medium heat for about 3 minutes, stirring constantly with a spatula, until the dough is sticky but not too runny.

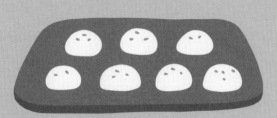

9

GLUTINOUS RICE FLOUR OR *MOCHIKO*

Don't try to prepare your mochi with another type of rice flour, because you won't be able to obtain the right consistency. That's where it got its name!

Chocolate hazelnut spread

MAKES 12 MOCHI

PREP TIME 5 MINUTES
FOR THE FILLING

REST TIME 40 MINUTES

1 Mochi dough (page 8)

*180 g (6½ oz) chocolate
hazelnut spread*

*1 teaspoon cornflour
(cornstarch)*

1 **PREPARE THE FILLING**

Spread a sheet of baking paper on a small plate and form 12 small mounds of chocolate hazelnut spread, about 15 g (½ oz) each. Freeze for 10 minutes.

2 **SHAPE THE FILLING**

Take the plate out and sprinkle it lightly with cornflour Roll the small mounds into balls and place them back in the freezer.

3 **PREPARE THE MOCHI DOUGH**

Make the mochi dough.

4 **FILL AND SHAPE THE MOCHI**

Place a very cold ball of filling on a disc of mochi dough Shape the mochi then place them in the fridge.

5 **LEAVE THE MOCHI TO REST BEFORE EATING**

Take the mochi out 30 minutes before eating to let them come to room temperature.

Caramelised walnut

MAKES 12 MOCHI	

PREP TIME 30 MINUTES
FOR THE FILLING

REST TIME 1 HOUR

---

1 Mochi dough (page 8)

60 g (2 oz) walnuts

60 g (2 oz) sugar

100 g (3½ oz) mascarpone

*1 teaspoon cornflour
(cornstarch)*

1. PREPARE THE FILLING

Mix the walnuts with the sugar and 50 ml (1¾ fl oz) of water in a small saucepan. Bring to the boil and let cook for 10–15 minutes until the liquid caramelises and turns brown. Pour onto a baking tray lined with baking paper and let cool. Chop 80 g (2¾ oz) of the caramelised walnuts and mix them with the mascarpone.

Spread a sheet of baking paper on a small plate and form 12 small dollops of the mascarpone walnuts. Freeze for 30 minutes.

2. SHAPE THE FILLING

Take the plate out of the freezer and sprinkle it lightly with cornflour. Roll the little mounds into balls and put them back in the freezer.

3. PREPARE THE MOCHI DOUGH

Make the mochi dough.

4. FILL AND SHAPE THE MOCHI

Place a cold ball of filling on a disc of mochi dough. Shape the mochi then place them in the fridge to chill.

5. LEAVE THE MOCHI TO REST BEFORE EATING

Take the mochi out 30 minutes before eating to let them come to room temperature.

Dango

110 g (4 oz) glutinous
rice flour

80 ml (⅓ cup) cold water

Sauce

40 g (1½ oz) caster
(superfine) sugar

40 ml (1¼ fl oz) water

1 tablespoon soy sauce

1 teaspoon cornflour
(cornstarch)

 PREPARE THE SAUCE

Combine the sauce ingredients in a small saucepan
and cook over medium heat for about 3 minutes,
stirring until the sauce coats the spoon well. Let cool
to room temperature.

 PREPARE THE MOCHI DOUGH

In a bowl, mix the glutinous rice flour with the water
and knead with your fingers to obtain a soft dough.

 SHAPE THE DANGO

Form a roll of about 25 cm (10 in) with the dough and
cut into 16 equal pieces. Roll the pieces into balls.

 COOK THE DANGO

Boil a large saucepan of water and drop the balls, one b
one, into the simmering water for 3 minutes. Gently tos
the balls to prevent them from sticking to the bottom
of the pan. Drain and then plunge the balls into very
cold water. Drain again.

 GLAZE BEFORE EATING

Thread 2 balls on each skewer and cover them with
sauce before serving.

Speculoos

MAKES 12 MOCHI

PREP TIME 10 MINUTES
FOR THE FILLING

REST TIME 1 HOUR

1 Mochi dough (page 8)

*½ teaspoon ground
cinnamon*

90 g (3 oz) mascarpone

*90 g (3 oz) speculoos
spread*

*1 teaspoon cornflour
(cornstarch)*

1 PREPARE THE FILLING

Mix the mascarpone with the speculoos paste in a small bowl until well combined.

Spread a sheet of baking paper on a small plate and form 12 small dollops of the mixture. Freeze for 30 minutes.

2 SHAPE THE FILLING

Take the plate out and sprinkle it lightly with cornflour. Form the small mounds into balls and put them back in the freezer.

3 PREPARE THE MOCHI DOUGH

Make the mochi dough by adding the cinnamon at the same time as the flour.

4 FILL AND SHAPE THE MOCHI

Place a very cold ball of filling on a disc of mochi dough. Shape the mochi then place them in the fridge.

5 LEAVE THE MOCHI TO REST BEFORE EATING

Take the mochi out 30 minutes before eating to let them come to room temperature.

Honey rose almond

MAKES 12 MOCHI
PREP TIME 5 MINUTES FOR THE FILLING
REST TIME 1 HOUR

1 Mochi dough (page 8)

red food colouring

100 g (1 cup) almond flour

30 g (1 oz) almond butter

20 g (¾ oz) flavoured honey (such as lavender or chestnut)

30 g (¼ cup) icing (confectioners') sugar

20 ml (¾ fl oz) water

2 drops rose water

1 teaspoon cornflour (cornstarch)

 PREPARE THE FILLING

Mix the almond flour with the almond butter, honey, icing sugar, water and rose water.

Spread a sheet of baking paper on a small plate and form 12 small heaps of the mixture. Freeze for 30 minutes.

 SHAPE THE FILLING

Take the plate out and sprinkle it lightly with cornflour. Roll the little mounds into balls and put them back in the freezer.

 PREPARE THE MOCHI DOUGH

Make the mochi dough by adding the colouring after the water and adjusting the quantity to obtain the desired colour.

 FILL AND SHAPE THE MOCHI

Place a very cold ball of filling on a disc of mochi dough. Shape the mochi then place them in the fridge.

 LEAVE THE MOCHI TO REST BEFORE EATING

Take the mochi out 30 minutes before eating to let them come to room temperature.

Orange blossom apricot

MAKES 12 MOCHI
PREP TIME 10 MINUTES FOR THE FILLING
REST TIME 1 HOUR

1 Mochi dough (page 8)

red food colouring

yellow food colouring

1 halved fresh apricot or 2 tinned apricot halves, drained

60 g (2 oz) almond flour

60 g (2 oz) mascarpone

1 teaspoon sugar

1 teaspoon orange blossom water

1 teaspoon cornflour (cornstarch)

 PREPARE THE FILLING

Cut the apricot halves into 5 mm (¼ in) dice. Mix the apricot with the almond flour, mascarpone, sugar and orange blossom water.

Spread a sheet of baking paper on a small plate and form 12 small heaps of the mixture. Freeze for 30 minutes.

 SHAPE THE FILLING

Take the plate out and sprinkle it lightly with cornflour. Roll the little mounds into balls and put them back in the freezer.

 PREPARE THE MOCHI DOUGH

Make the mochi dough by adding the food colouring after the water and adjusting the quantities to obtain the desired colour.

 FILL AND SHAPE THE MOCHI

Place a very cold ball of filling on a disc of mochi dough. Shape the mochi then place them in the fridge.

 LEAVE THE MOCHI TO REST BEFORE EATING

Take the mochi out 30 minutes before eating to let them come to room temperature.

Raspberry ice cream

MAKES 12 MOCHI

PREP TIME 5 MINUTES
FOR THE FILLING

REST TIME
2 HOURS 30 MINUTES
+ 2 HOURS

---

1 Mochi dough (page 8)

red food colouring

60 g (2 oz) cream cheese

100 g (3½ oz) raspberries

*1 sachet (7.5 g/¼ oz)
vanilla sugar*

*1 teaspoon cornflour
(cornstarch)*

 PREPARE THE FILLING

Mash the cream cheese with the raspberries and vanilla sugar.

Spread a sheet of baking paper on a small plate and form 12 small heaps of filling. Freeze for 30 minutes.

 SHAPE THE FILLING

Take the plate out and sprinkle it lightly with cornflour. Roll the mounds into balls and place them back in the freezer for at least 2 hours.

 PREPARE THE MOCHI DOUGH

Make the mochi dough by adding the food colouring after the water and adjusting the quantity to obtain the desired colour.

 FILL AND SHAPE THE MOCHI

Place a very cold ball of filling on a disc of mochi dough. Shape the mochi and keep them cool. Be careful – your hands must be well sprinkled with cornflour so that the filling does not stick to your fingers. Place the mochi in the freezer for at least 2 hours.

 LEAVE THE MOCHI TO REST BEFORE EATING

Take the mochi out of the freezer 5 minutes before eating to soften them.

Sesame

MAKES 12 MOCHI	
PREP TIME 5 MINUTES FOR THE FILLING	
REST TIME 1 HOUR	

1 Mochi dough (page 8)

black food colouring (optional)

60 g (2 oz) almond flour

120 g (4½ oz) black or white tahini

20 g (¾ oz) icing (confectioners') sugar

1 teaspoon cornflour (cornstarch)

① PREPARE THE FILLING

Mix the almond flour with the tahini and icing sugar in a small bowl until combined.

Spread a sheet of baking paper on a small plate and form 12 small heaps of the mixture. Freeze for 30 minutes.

② SHAPE THE FILLING

Take the plate out and sprinkle it lightly with cornflour. Roll the little mounds into balls and put them back in the freezer.

③ PREPARE THE MOCHI DOUGH

Make the mochi dough by adding the colouring after the water, if using, and adjusting the quantity to obtain the desired colour.

④ FILL AND SHAPE THE MOCHI

Place a very cold ball of filling on a disc of mochi dough. Shape the mochi then place them in the fridge.

⑤ LEAVE THE MOCHI TO REST BEFORE EATING

Take the mochi out 30 minutes before eating to let them come to room temperature.

TIP

To make a mixture of black and white mochi, mix half of the mochi dough with black food colouring and cook the dough twice with the same cooking times.

For the filling, in a bowl, mix half of the icing sugar and almond flour with 60 g (2 oz) of black tahini, and the other half with 60 g (2 oz) of white tahini.

Fill the black mochi with white filling and the white mochi with black filling.

Chocolate

MAKES 12 MOCHI
PREP TIME 10 MINUTES FOR THE FILLING
REST TIME 1 HOUR 30 MINUTES

1 Mochi dough (page 8)

black food colouring

red food colouring

120 ml (4 fl oz) cream

60 g (2 oz) dark cooking
chocolate, chopped

1 teaspoon cornflour
(cornstarch)

1 pinch of unsweetened
cocoa powder

 PREPARE THE FILLING

Pour the cream into a saucepan, bring to the boil, then stop cooking immediately. Pour the chopped chocolate into the saucepan and allow to melt for 5 minutes without stirring. Mix, pour into a bowl and place in the fridge to chill for 30 minutes.

Spread a sheet of baking paper on a small plate and form 12 small heaps of the mixture. Freeze for 30 minutes.

 SHAPE THE FILLING

Take the plate out and sprinkle it lightly with cornflour. Roll the little mounds into balls and put them back in the freezer.

 PREPARE THE MOCHI DOUGH

Make the mochi dough by adding the food colouring after the water and adjusting the quantity to obtain the desired colour.

 FILL AND SHAPE THE MOCHI

Place a very cold ball of filling on a disc of mochi dough. Shape the mochi then place them in the fridge.

 LEAVE THE MOCHI TO REST BEFORE EATING

Take the mochi out 30 minutes before eating to let them come to room temperature. Sprinkle with the cocoa powder before serving.

Straw- berry

MAKES 12 MOCHI

PREP TIME
1 HOUR 45 MINUTES
FOR THE FILLING

REST TIME 1 HOUR

1 Mochi dough (page 8)

red food colouring

50 g (1¾ oz) adzuki beans

40 g (1½ oz) caster
(superfine) sugar

1 pinch of salt

12 small strawberries,
rinsed and hulled

1 PREPARE THE FILLING

Prepare the adzuki bean paste (with the beans, sugar and salt) as for the Anko mochi recipe (see page 45) and finely mash or blend it.

Spread a sheet of baking paper on a baking tray. Coat each strawberry with bean paste and arrange on the baking tray. You will normally only use half the bean paste. You can eat the rest or wrap it up and store it in the freezer for the next time you prepare mochi.

2 SHAPE THE FILLING

Place the strawberries in the fridge for 30 minutes.

3 PREPARE THE MOCHI DOUGH

Make the mochi dough by adding the food colouring after the water and adjusting the quantities to obtain the desired colour.

4 FILL AND SHAPE THE MOCHI

Place a very cold ball of filling on a disc of mochi dough. Shape the mochi then place them in the fridge.

5 LEAVE THE MOCHI TO REST BEFORE EATING

Take the mochi out 30 minutes before eating to let them come to room temperature.

Lemon

MAKES 12 MOCHI	
PREP TIME 15 MINUTES FOR THE FILLING	
REST TIME 3 HOURS	

1 Mochi dough (page 8)

zest of ½ lemon

1 egg

75 ml (2½ fl oz) full-cream (whole) milk

30 g (1 oz) caster (superfine) sugar

2 teaspoons cornflour (cornstarch)

30 ml (1 fl oz) lemon juice

PREPARE THE FILLING

In a small saucepan, whisk the egg with the milk, sugar, 1 teaspoon of the cornflour and then add the lemon juice.

Cook for about 3 minutes over medium heat until the cream coats the spoon.

Pour into a bowl and place in the fridge for 2 hours.

Spread a sheet of baking paper on a small plate and form 12 small heaps of the mixture. Freeze for 30 minutes.

SHAPE THE FILLING

Take the plate out and sprinkle it lightly with the rest of the cornflour. Roll the little mounds into balls and put them back in the freezer.

PREPARE THE MOCHI DOUGH

Make the mochi dough by adding the lemon zest along with the water.

FILL AND SHAPE THE MOCHI

Place a very cold ball of filling on a disc of mochi dough. Shape the mochi then place them in the fridge.

LEAVE THE MOCHI TO REST BEFORE EATING

Take the mochi out 30 minutes before eating to let them come to room temperature.

FUN FACTS

We pronounce it **MO(T)CHI**,
not to be confused with *moshi moshi*, which
means 'hello' in Japanese.

•

Mochi originated in **China**
and were brought to **Japan**
2000 years ago.

•

Please note: enjoy your mochi
in small bites (3 or 4 ideally).
Don't gulp them down even though they're
delicious – a whole mochi is too sticky
to swallow at once!

•

The consistency of a mochi is as supple, soft
and plump as **a baby's cheek**!

Vanilla

MAKES 12 MOCHI
PREP TIME 5 MINUTES FOR THE FILLING
REST TIME 1 HOUR

1 Mochi dough (page 8)

black food colouring

170 g (6 oz) mascarpone

1 sachet (7.5 g/¼ oz) vanilla sugar

1 teaspoon cornflour (cornstarch)

 PREPARE THE FILLING

Mix the mascarpone with the vanilla sugar.
Spread a sheet of baking paper on a small plate and form 12 small heaps of the mixture. Freeze for 30 minutes.

 SHAPE THE FILLING

Take the plate out and sprinkle it lightly with cornflour. Roll the little mounds into balls and put them back in the freezer.

 PREPARE THE MOCHI DOUGH

Make the mochi dough by adding the food colouring after the water and adjusting the quantity to obtain the desired colour.

 FILL AND SHAPE THE MOCHI

Place a very cold ball of filling on a disc of mochi dough Shape the mochi then place them in the fridge.

 LEAVE THE MOCHI TO REST BEFORE EATING

Take the mochi out 30 minutes before eating to let them come to room temperature.

Peanut butter jelly

MAKES 12 MOCHI	

PREP TIME 10 MINUTES
FOR THE FILLING

REST TIME 1 HOUR

---

1 Mochi dough (page 8)

red food colouring

12 raspberries

*120 g (4½ oz) peanut
butter*

*1 teaspoon cornflour
(cornstarch)*

1 PREPARE THE FILLING

Gently coat each raspberry with some peanut butter.

Spread a sheet of baking paper on a small plate and place the coated raspberries on the sheet, then transfer them to the fridge to chill for for 30 minutes.

2 SHAPE THE FILLING

Take the plate out and sprinkle it lightly with cornflour. Roll the coated raspberries into balls and place them back into the fridge.

3 PREPARE THE MOCHI DOUGH

Make the mochi dough.

4 FILL AND SHAPE THE MOCHI

Place each coated raspberry on a disc of mochi dough. Shape the mochi then place them in the fridge.

5 LEAVE THE MOCHI TO REST BEFORE EATING

Take the mochi out 30 minutes before eating to let them come to room temperature.

Hazelnut and chestnut

MAKES 12 MOCHI

PREP TIME 5 MINUTES
FOR THE FILLING

REST TIME 1 HOUR

1 Mochi dough (page 8)

1 teaspoon unsweetened
cocoa powder

90 g (3 oz) hazelnut puree

90 g (3 oz) chestnut cream

1 teaspoon cornflour
(cornstarch)

 PREPARE THE FILLING

Mix the hazelnut puree with the chestnut cream.
Spread a sheet of baking paper on a small plate
and form 12 small heaps of the mixture. Freeze for
30 minutes.

 SHAPE THE FILLING

Take the plate out and sprinkle it lightly with cornflour.
Roll the little mounds into balls and put them back in
the freezer.

 PREPARE THE MOCHI DOUGH

Make the mochi dough by adding the cocoa at the same
time as the flour.

 FILL AND SHAPE THE MOCHI

Place a very cold ball of filling on a disc of mochi dough.
Shape the mochi then place them in the fridge.

 LEAVE THE MOCHI TO REST BEFORE EATING

Take the mochi out 30 minutes before eating to let
them come to room temperature.

Anko* mochi

MAKES 12 MOCHI
PREP TIME 1 HOUR 30 MINUTES FOR THE FILLING
REST TIME 1 HOUR

1 Mochi dough (page 8)

50 g (1¾ oz) adzuki beans

40 g (1½ oz) caster (superfine) sugar

1 pinch of salt

* ADZUKI BEAN PASTE

1. PREPARE THE FILLING

Rinse the beans and pour them into a saucepan with 150 ml (5 fl oz) of cold water. Bring to the boil, add 250 ml (1 cup) of cold water, wait for the water to reboil and cook for a further 2 minutes.

Drain and rinse the beans and the pan (remove the black deposits). Put the beans back in the saucepan with 150 ml (5 fl oz) of cold water, bring to the boil and cook for 10 minutes. Rinse the beans and the pan again. The purpose of this is to remove the bitterness from the beans.

Pour the beans back into the pan and add 250 ml (1 cup) of cold water. Bring to the boil, then lower the heat and simmer for about 1 hour 15 minutes, adding a little cold water during cooking if it evaporates too much.

At the end of cooking, there should be water just to the level of the beans. Add half of the sugar and stir while continuing to cook.

When there is almost no more liquid, add the rest of the sugar and the salt, cook while stirring for another 3–4 minutes.

You can use the whole beans for the filling or mix everything to obtain a slightly grainy paste.

2. SHAPE THE FILLING

Spread a sheet of baking paper on a small plate and form 12 small heaps of the adzuki bean mixture on the sheet. Freeze for 30 minutes.

3. PREPARE THE MOCHI DOUGH

Make the mochi dough.

4. FILL AND SHAPE THE MOCHI

Place a very cold ball of filling on a disc of mochi dough. Shape the mochi then place them in the fridge.

5. LEAVE THE MOCHI TO REST BEFORE EATING

Take the mochi out 30 minutes before eating to let them come to room temperature.

Blueberry lemon

MAKES 12 MOCHI
PREP TIME 10 MINUTES FOR THE FILLING
REST TIME 1 HOUR

1 Mochi dough (page 8)

red food colouring

blue food colouring

100 g (3½ oz) mascarpone

1 teaspoon icing (confectioners') sugar

zest of ¼ lemon

12 blueberries

1 teaspoon cornflour (cornstarch)

 PREPARE THE FILLING

Mix the mascarpone with the icing sugar and lemon zest.
Spread a sheet of baking paper on a small plate and form 12 small heaps of mascarpone on the sheet. Press a blueberry in the centre of each and cover with more mascarpone. Freeze for 30 minutes.

 SHAPE THE FILLING

Take the plate out and sprinkle it lightly with cornflour. Roll the little mounds into balls and put them back in the freezer.

 PREPARE THE MOCHI DOUGH

Make the mochi dough by adding the food colouring after the water and adjusting the quantities to obtain the desired colour.

 FILL AND SHAPE THE MOCHI

Place a very cold ball of filling on a disc of mochi dough. Shape the mochi then place them in the fridge.

 LEAVE THE MOCHI TO REST BEFORE EATING

Take the mochi out 30 minutes before eating to let them come to room temperature.

Coconut mango

MAKES 12 MOCHI
PREP TIME 10 MINUTES FOR THE FILLING
REST TIME 1 HOUR

1 Mochi dough (page 8)

yellow food colouring

blue food colouring

100 g (3½ oz) mango flesh

20 g (¾ oz) icing (confectioners') sugar

½ teaspoon agar-agar

100 ml (3½ fl oz) coconut cream

1 PREPARE THE FILLING

Mix the mango flesh with the icing sugar, agar-agar and coconut cream. Bring to the boil, stirring, then boil for 1 minute, stirring constantly. Pour into a bowl and place in the freezer for at least 30 minutes until firm.

2 SHAPE THE FILLING

Turn out the mango mixture from the bowl, roughly shape and then cut into 12 cubes. Put the cubes back in the freezer.

3 PREPARE THE MOCHI DOUGH

Make the mochi dough by adding the food colouring after the water and adjusting the quantities to obtain the desired colour.

4 SHAPE AND FILL THE MOCHI

Place a very cold cube of the filling on a disc of mochi dough. Shape the mochi then place them in the fridge.

5 LEAVE THE MOCHI TO REST BEFORE EATING

Take the mochi out 30 minutes before eating to let them come to room temperature.

Matcha coconut

MAKES 12 MOCHI

PREP TIME 10 MINUTES
FOR THE FILLING

REST TIME
1 HOUR 30 MINUTES

1 Mochi dough (page 8)

1 teaspoon matcha tea

120 ml (4 fl oz) cream

60 g (2 oz) white cooking chocolate, chopped

1 teaspoon cornflour (cornstarch)

2 tablespoons desiccated coconut

 PREPARE THE FILLING

For the filling, sift ½ teaspoon of the matcha tea into a bowl. Pour the cream over the matcha tea, little by little, stirring constantly so that the tea is well diluted.

Pour the mixture into a saucepan and bring to the boil. Once boiling, stop cooking immediately, then pour the chopped chocolate into the saucepan and let it melt for 5 minutes without stirring. Mix through, then pour into a bowl and place it in the fridge for 30 minutes.

Spread a sheet of baking paper on a small plate and form 12 small heaps of the mixture on the sheet. Freeze for 30 minutes.

 SHAPE THE FILLING

Take the plate out and sprinkle it lightly with cornflour. Roll the little mounds into balls and put them back in the freezer.

 PREPARE THE MOCHI DOUGH

Make the mochi dough by adding the rest of the sifted matcha tea at the same time as the flour.

 SHAPE AND FILL THE MOCHI

Place a very cold ball of filling on a disc of mochi dough. Sprinkle the coconut onto a plate. Shape the mochi then roll each one in the coconut. Place them in the fridge.

 LEAVE THE MOCHI TO REST BEFORE EATING

Take the mochi out 30 minutes before eating to let them come to room temperature.

Praline coffee

1 Mochi dough (page 8)

1 teaspoon unsweetened cocoa powder

120 g (4½ oz) mascarpone

30 g (1 oz) praline paste

20 g (⅓ cup) instant coffee

20 g (¾ oz) icing (confectioners') sugar

1 teaspoon cornflour (cornstarch)

1 PREPARE THE FILLING

Mix the mascarpone with the praline paste, instant coffee and icing sugar.

Spread a sheet of baking paper on a small plate and form 12 small heaps of the mixture on the sheet. Place them in the freezer for 30 minutes.

2 SHAPE THE FILLING

Take the plate out and sprinkle it lightly with cornflour. Roll the little mounds into balls and put them back in the freezer.

3 PREPARE THE MOCHI DOUGH

Make the mochi dough by adding the cocoa at the same time as the flour.

4 FILL AND SHAPE THE MOCHI

Place a very cold ball of the filling on a disc of mochi dough. Shape the mochi then place them in the fridge.

5 LEAVE THE MOCHI TO REST BEFORE EATING

Take the mochi out 30 minutes before eating to let them come to room temperature.

Mochi

Mochi or *mochi gome* (literally 'glutinous rice') is the name
given to the rice used to make the dough. The mochi that are
eaten filled are *daifuku mochi*. Mochi dough balls are *dango
mochi*. The mochi dough is stuffed with a filling. Traditionally,
it is a sweet red bean paste, called *anko*, but it can also be
fresh fruit or other sweet and/or frozen preparations.

Black sesame matcha

MAKES 12 MOCHI

PREP TIME 5 MINUTES
FOR THE FILLING

REST TIME 1 HOUR

1 Mochi dough (page 8)

1 teaspoon matcha tea

*1 teaspoon black
sesame seeds*

60 g (2 oz) almond flour

120 g (4½ oz) black tahini

*20 g (¾ oz) icing
(confectioners') sugar*

*1 teaspoon cornflour
(cornstarch)*

 PREPARE THE FILLING

Mix the almond flour with the tahini and icing sugar.

Spread a sheet of baking paper on a small plate and form 12 small heaps of the mixture on the sheet. Place them in the freezer for 30 minutes.

 SHAPE THE FILLING

Take the plate out and sprinkle it lightly with cornflour Roll the little mounds into balls and put them back in the freezer.

 PREPARE THE MOCHI DOUGH

Make the mochi dough by adding the sifted matcha tea and sesame seeds along with the flour.

 SHAPE AND FILL THE MOCHI

Place a very cold ball of filling on a disc of mochi dough Shape the mochi then place them in the fridge.

 LEAVE THE MOCHI TO REST BEFORE EATING

Take the mochi out 30 minutes before eating to let them come to room temperature.

Passionfruit

MAKES 12 MOCHI
PREP TIME 10 MINUTES FOR THE FILLING
REST TIME 1 HOUR

1 Mochi dough (page 8)

yellow food colouring

120 g (4½ oz) strained passionfruit pulp

½ teaspoon agar-agar

60 g (2 oz) sweetened condensed milk

 PREPARE THE FILLING

Mix the passionfruit pulp with the agar-agar and sweetened condensed milk in a saucepan. Bring to the boil, stirring, then boil for 1 minute, stirring constantly. Pour into a bowl and place in the freezer for at least 30 minutes.

 SHAPE THE FILLING

Turn the mixture out from the bowl, cut into 12 cubes and place back in the freezer.

 PREPARE THE MOCHI DOUGH

Make the mochi dough by adding the food colouring at the same time as the water and adjusting the quantity to obtain the desired colour.

 FILL AND SHAPE THE MOCHI

Place a very cold ball of filling on a disc of mochi dough. Shape the mochi then place them in the fridge.

 LEAVE THE MOCHI TO REST BEFORE EATING

Take the mochi out 30 minutes before eating to let them come to room temperature.

ice cream mochi

MAKES 12 MOCHI

PREP TIME 5 MINUTES
FOR THE FILLING

REST TIME 8 HOURS

1 Mochi dough (page 8)

red food colouring

blue food colouring

yellow food colouring

*4 scoops vanilla ice cream
(15 g/½ oz each)*

*4 scoops chocolate ice
cream (15 g/½ oz each)*

*4 scoops strawberry
ice cream or sorbet
(15 g/½ oz each)*

*1 teaspoon cornflour
(cornstarch), plus extra
for coating*

① PREPARE THE FILLING

Roll each scoop of ice cream in cornflour to coat well and place on a baking tray lined with baking paper. Freeze for at least 5 hours.

② SHAPE THE FILLING

After 5 hours, take out the ice cream scoops and roll them again in cornflour. Return to the freezer for a further 1 hour.

③ PREPARE THE MOCHI DOUGH

Make the mochi dough by adding the food colouring after the water and adjusting the quantity to obtain the desired colour.

④ FILL AND SHAPE THE MOCHI

Place a scoop of ice cream on a disc of mochi dough.

Take care that your hands are well sprinkled with cornflour so that the filling does not stick to your fingers, then shape the mochi and keep them cool. Place the mochi in the freezer for at least 2 hours.

⑤ LEAVE THE MOCHI TO REST BEFORE EATING

Take the mochi out 5 minutes before serving so that they soften.

TIP

To make the three different colours of mochi, mix one-third of the dough with red colouring to obtain pink, one-third with a little yellow and blue colouring to obtain green, and keep one-third of the dough plain. Cook the dough in 3 parts, reducing the cooking time by 15 seconds for each period in the microwave.

Alternatively, spread each piece of mochi dough on small squares of plastic wrap (10 × 10 cm/4 × 4 in each), place a scoop of ice cream in the centre of a circle of dough. Pinch the excess plastic wrap at the corners and lift them together to gather the dough around the scoop of ice cream. Twist the wrap to create a tight ball. Place the plastic wrap–covered mochi in the freezer and remove the wrap before serving.

TO ENJOY AT TEA TIME

Mochi is best enjoyed with a tea: a sencha green tea, genmaicha (green tea with puffed rice) or a sobacha (infusion of grilled buckwheat), a matcha latte (powdered green tea), or even a light Earl Grey tea, the mochi's sweetness counterbalancing the bitterness of the tea.

Mochi can accompany both an iced coffee and a hot coffee with milk (cappuccino, macchiato or café latte).

For a more sophisticated combination, serve the mochi with a glass of champagne or sparkling wine.

First published in French by Hachette Livre (Marabout) in 2023
Hachette Book 58, rue Jean-Bleuzen 92178 Vanves Cedex

This edition published in 2024 by Smith Street Books
Naarm (Melbourne) | Australia
smithstreetbooks.com

ISBN: 978-1-9227-5497-4

Smith Street Books respectfully acknowledges the Wurundjeri People of the Kulin Nation, who are the Traditional Owners of the land on which we work, and we pay our respects to their Elders past and present.

The moral right of the author has been asserted.

For Hachette Livre (Marabout)
Proofreading: Emilie Collet
Layout: Nicolas Gally
Stylist: Sabrina Fauda-Role
Illustrations: Valentine Ferrandi

For Smith Street Books
Publisher: Paul McNally
Translation: Lucy Grant
Editor: Ariana Klepac
Production Manager: Aisling Coughlan
Proofreader: Pam Dunne

Printed & bound in China

Book 302
10 9 8 7 6 5 4 3 2 1